~ THE ~
GREATEST
DAYS ARE
AHEAD!

THE GREATEST DAYS ARE AHEAD!

JOSEPH CLEVELAND RODRIGUEZ, JR.

Foreword

by Andrew Shearman

I happily commend this study and reflection from Joseph Rodriguez. Joseph has made the journey from lawlessness, through religious legalism, to freedom in Christ through love, mercy, and grace. I have been privileged to watch and be part of this pilgrimage and have always been blessed by Joseph's hunger for truth and his amazing capacity to absorb and recall Scripture and, very importantly, to allow himself to be changed by the Truth.

Joseph is a passionate and honest seeker after truth, who lets the Bible interpret the Bible and, with the help of the abiding Presence of Holy Spirit in his life, is "led into all Truth" — the *logos* and *rhema* in glorious harmony, pointing us always back to Jesus Christ Himself. Check out the Scriptures for yourself and allow Holy Spirit to guide you — your life will be enriched, your legacy ensured, and the generations impacted.

Contents

Introduction

J oseph Cleveland Rodriguez, Jr., was born in Bayou La Batre, Alabama, on January 24, 1956, christened Catholic after birth at Saint Margaret's Catholic Church in Bayou La Batre, afterward I was raised in San Souci Baptist Church, accepted the Lord around age 12, and was baptized there, at San Souci Baptist. As far as schooling is concerned, I attended Alba School in Bayou La Batre, Alabama, for 12 years and graduated in 1974, then attended schooling as an electrical apprentice in Local 505 of the IBEW, became a boat builder in 1977 with my parents' help, and have remained in the boat-building business to this day.

I Didn't Get What I Deserved

I consider my life a testament to the grace of God, and feel the need to "puke out" some of my not-so-good past. After eight years of marriage, my first wife and I divorced; I was no doubt the main cause of that break up. I smoked a bit of pot, partied, bar hopped, and headed down the wrong path for a while. Somehow, in the midst of my stupidity and selfish mistakes, I know that God was there all along. He has been relentless in His pursuit of my soul and never gives up on us.

My wife, Patricia, and I will celebrate our 34-year anniversary in July 2016. A few months after we married, we began to talk about our Christian faith and we both got back into church and served under my Baptist pastor over three years at San Souci Baptist Church in Bayou La Batre, Alabama, where

I was raised. I played the organ during worship and soon began to teach the young adult Sunday school class. My wife taught the 10-12 year old's in Sunday school as well. That teaching caused me to prepare the lesson each Sunday and therefore learn the Scriptures well enough to ask questions which were not easy for my pastor to answer. I found myself driven to search out the truth as I was not satisfied with many of the answers I got.

My wife and I saw her mother and father saved (they had been alcoholics for the whole of my wife's life), along with many other great things God did. A few years later, her dad died and I preached his funeral and, a few more years later, both her mother and my mother died on the same day, within 30 minutes of each other. I also preached their funerals, my mom's was the day before Thanksgiving and my wife's mom was the day after Thanksgiving. This was another difficult time in my life, but it reinforced the thought that my wife and I were destined to be together. Some way, somehow, God knew all along and He blessed a broken road in my life' that's what He came to do for us all.

After I received the baptism in the Holy Spirit, I started a Thursday-night Bible study at our house. We saw several saved and even baptized them in the bayou just behind our home. Needless to say, we knew our time would be short-lived at the Baptist church as the word got out regarding our spiritual baptism, but we patiently waited for word from the Lord. By the way, when I use the terms "spiritual baptism," "spirit baptism," or "baptism in the Holy Spirit," I'm speaking of the same thing. Please consider all of these various references as synonyms while you read my book. My spiritual baptism happened over a decade *after* my water baptism. However, the pattern in Scripture is that our spiritual baptism should be at the same time as our water baptism.

It was only a couple more months, until one morning as we were getting ready for service, I heard the Lord say, "Today is the day."

After service that day, I pulled my pastor aside and told him we would be leaving the church that day, but not on any bad terms at all.

Brother Evans asked me, "Where are you going to go?"

I replied, "I don't know."

He then asked, "How can you leave and not know where you're going?"

I replied, "I guess like Abraham, I'm going out, not knowing where, and I'm looking for a city which has foundations, whose builder and maker is God."

I'm happy to say that my Baptist pastor, Bryce Evans, invited me to preach a couple times, even after we had left the church. Brother Evans is still alive, still pastoring, and still my friend. You cannot move into any new area of ministry carrying bad baggage from your former place!

About a week later, we rented an old Methodist church building in town and started a fellowship with a handful of folks. The Saturday before our first service, one of the ladies who had a bit of a prophetic gift, stopped the vacuum cleaner she was using and was standing there staring at the back wall of the sanctuary. I noticed her and knew something was up, so I asked her what was going on.

She said, "I see a scripture on the back wall," and I asked her what she saw.

She said, "He looked for a city that hath foundations, whose builder and maker is God."

I hadn't told anyone what I had just said to my pastor a few days before. Wow! So, we put that scripture on the wall and I began 25 years of ministry. After a few years, we bought land in west Mobile, Alabama, and constructed a new church building. I was privileged to meet and befriend several wonderful men and women of God, who were needed influences on my life. We saw the church grow to just over a hundred folks and we accomplished a few memorable victories for the cause of Christ.

Through the ups and downs of church ministry and my lack of leadership, along with my "open" freedom to enjoy a glass of wine or alcoholic beverage, the church went stagnate somewhat and the numbers began to fall off. No doubt, I was the main cause of the church going down to the point of us deciding to sell the assets, which we did, to another local fellowship who needed a facility to meet in. We gave them a great deal on the building and also gave all the money away to various Christian ministries, both local and international. My wife and I currently are members of South Coast Church in Mobile and have no plans otherwise, but to serve and support the ministry there.

I wondered if I should share a synopsis of my life, as this book was not intended to be about me, but one of my great ministry friends, Mike Paschall, whom has already published a few books, advised me to. He said it would "put a human touch" to my words. So there it is, the short story of a seemingly failed ministry leader. Maybe this will help some of you reading this book to know that God can and will use anyone He chooses. I don't qualify to write a book, but He has pushed me to do it for years and I pray my words will bring hope and life to all who consider what I have to say.

I am by no means what you would envision a Christian book writer to look like. My life has seen repeated stupidities and sin by me. Most of my Fundamentalist brothers avoided me due to my being baptized in the Holy Spirit and my Pentecostal brothers avoided me due to my open freedom to enjoy alcoholic beverages. I did not get what I deserved from God, and for that I say, "Thank God."

Today, I have four daughters, Mandy and April (from my first marriage), Hannah and Hope (by my current wife). Three of them are nurses and one is educated in psychology. Two grandsons, Craig Michael Harrell and Roman Stanford Harrington, with a third one, Tucker Cale Bosarge, due in early in 2016. Three granddaughters, Randi and Rachel Tillman (twins), and Savannah Strous. My baby daughter, Hope, who is 24 is not currently married and has no children, so I'm sure to have other grands to come.

My wife is and has been a gift from heaven for me. She is an awesome woman of God, mother, grandmother, friend to many, and continues to keep me on the right path. One of my greatest hopes for this book is that, after I'm dead and gone, my progeny down the line, who never knew me in person, will catch my spirit in these words and see my total dependency on the grace of God and how great that grace is!

He used a Canaanite harlot named Rahab, a Moabite woman named Ruth, a Hittite woman named Bathsheba, and they all three birthed the progeny of Jesus Christ Himself! That's right! Their genes were in the earthly parents of Jesus! It's never been about blood lineage; it's always been about faith! No matter what you've done or what's been done to you, God loves to put broken lives back together and He has a great future and hope planned for us all. He came to seek and save that which was lost and I qualified!

During my 25 years of ministry, I gave myself to the study of eschatology (end-time events) and feel I have something to say that's worth saying on that subject! I know, most Christians could care less about eschatology, maybe you'll change your mind a bit after reading this book. Whether we realize it or not, a lot of what we believe is directly connected to our understanding of end-time events.

I want to deal with several topics in Scripture as I lay the foundation to build a conclusion on. My intention is to show clear scriptural and historical evidence from which this book's title originated. I highly recommend that you have your Bible handy and read the passages I've listed as we take this journey together. First off, I want to clarify something; my belief that the greatest days are ahead is not dependent on my personal life. No matter what happens to me, my family, or even my country, the greatest days are ahead for the spread of the Gospel of Jesus Christ and for the Kingdom of God filling all things.

Resources

I mostly quote the King James Bible, but also use the Amplified Bible periodically. I will also be quoting from Josephus, a Jewish historian, who was an eyewitness to many events surrounding the 70 AD time period. I've read several great books which have influenced and helped me gain understanding and will periodically quote from them as well. And, I must mention, there have been many men and women of God who have helped mold me along the way. No doubt, their influence will periodically show itself.

"It would be easy to show that at our present rate of progress, the kingdoms of this world could never become the kingdom of our Lord and of His Christ. Indeed, many in the Church are giving up the idea of it except on the occasion of the advent of Christ, which, as it chimes in with our own idleness, is likely to be a popular doctrine. I myself believe that King Jesus will reign, and the idols be utterly abolished; but I expect the same power which turned the world upside down once will still continue to do it. The Holy Ghost would never suffer the imputation to rest upon His holy name that He was not able to convert the world." — *Charles Haddon Spurgeon, 1834-1892*

List of Topics

A. The Tabernacle of David: Amos 9:11-12, Acts 15:5-19, Isaiah 16:5
B. Daniel's 70-Weeks Prophecy: Daniel 9:24-27, Ezra 1:1-2, Isaiah 44:28 and 45:1
C. The Feast of Tabernacles: Deuteronomy 16:16, Psalm 89:15
D. The Dating of the Writing of Revelation: Revelation 17:10
E. The Olivet Discourse: Matthew 24, Mark 13, Luke 13
F. The Rock: Daniel 2

The Tabernacle
of David

The Tabernacle of David

L et's get started with the Tabernacle of David. I realize most Christians know little or nothing about the Tabernacle of David. It's not a subject I heard anything about until I was in my mid-twenties. I went to Sunday school almost every Sunday as a kid. It was there all along but I never heard a sermon involving the Tabernacle of David, however, over the last 20 years I've heard a bit more on this topic, and so we should!

Background

When David became king, the Ark of the Covenant had been lost to the Philistines under the previous administration (Saul's). On the first attempt, David made mistakes in his efforts to recover the Ark and Uzza died (2 Samuel 6). David left the Ark in Obed-Edom's house (a Gentile) for three months because David didn't know what to do with it. As time went on, David learned that the Lord had blessed the Gentile and his household because of the presence of Ark. David inquired of the Lord and realized that they had tried to carry the Ark on a cart rather than on the "shoulders of the sanctified priesthood." When David went back again to recover the Ark from Obed-Edom, he brought it to Mount Zion and placed it under an open tent where everyone could see it and worship before it. I Chronicles 15:1 says that David *"pitched a tent"* for the Ark of the Lord. The Ark stayed in the Tabernacle of David for about 40 years!

Recovering the Ark

On his way up Zion with the Ark of the Lord, David was dancing and playing before the Lord dressed only in a priestly ephod and his undergarments (I Chronicles 15:25-29). Talk about a "new thing." We see in verse 29 that David's wife (Saul's daughter), Michal saw David dancing and playing before all the people in his "Fruit of the Looms" and she despised him for it! In 2 Samuel 6, we find the same story being told, but in verses 20-23, Samuel adds that when David returned home to bless his house, his wife (Michal)confronted David with her words of disgust and outrage over his public humiliation. David quickly set her straight with his own words and the exchange between David and Michal ended with the scripture saying in verse 23, *"Therefore Michal, the daughter of Saul, had no child unto the day of her death"!*

It doesn't say she was barren, so apparently, David had no intimacy with her from that time forward! That's thought provoking, to say the least. I'm careful about reading things into Scripture, but it seems to me that if you want intimacy with the King, you best not scoff at someone worshiping the Lord in a way that may seem to be a bit strange to you. Be careful about such scoffing.

David Sets Up the "Order of Service"

After the initial dedication ceremonies for the Ark, there were no more animal sacrifices! David had both Jew and Gentile there! Obed-Edom was on the staff, he was a doorkeeper at the Tabernacle of David. Other Gentiles were also given access! David instituted music, singers, dancing, and wrote a lot of the psalms under the influence of the Holy Spirit's presence which was there. By the way, over on Mount Gibeon, about seven miles north of Jerusalem, the Tabernacle of Moses was in full operation with priest and sacrifices, but they had no Ark behind the veil. Hmmm?

David did not bring the Ark back to the Tabernacle of Moses and replace it in the Holy of Holies, even though the Tabernacle of Moses was in full operation! Wow! Did David presume on God? I think not, or he wouldn't have lived. Did David "see" 1,500 years ahead of time, a glimpse of where God was going?

David's Prophetic Insight

David wrote in Psalm 141:2, *"Let my prayer be set forth before thee as incense; and the lifting of my hands as the evening sacrifice."* There were no incense burners there, no sacrifices there, but David saw the reality of what those "shadows" represented! I suggest, as always, go read the story for yourselves, in 2 Samuel 6 and 1 Chronicles 15 and 16. This was a big deal, especially when you consider the exclusion of Gentiles from the Tabernacle of Moses, and the Gentiles' access to the Tabernacle of David.

Solomon Builds the Temple

We know that David's son, Solomon, went on to build the first Temple, where the Ark was moved in later years (see 1 Kings 8). In 2 Chronicles

7:6, we find that when Solomon set up the order of service in the Temple, he carried his father David's musical instruments right on in! Wow, the Mosaic order of service was augmented by Tabernacle-of-David worship, which was brought in by Solomon! We also know from history that the Ark was lost some time after the Babylonians destroyed the Temple and took Daniel and other young Hebrew men to Babylon as captives (we'll talk a lot about Daniel later, in the 70-weeks topic).

The last mention of the Ark in the Old Testament is found in Jeremiah 3:16-17: *"And it shall come to pass, when ye be multiplied and increased in the land, in those days, saith the Lord, they shall say no more, The Ark of the Covenant of the Lord: neither shall it come to mind: neither shall they remember it; neither shall they visit it; neither shall that be done anymore."* Therefore, we should disregard any hoopla such as movies about finding the Ark. Christ has fulfilled the role which the Ark played in the Old Covenant — seek Him, not some gold-plated box which was but a shadow!

The First Church Council Meeting

So, let's move forward about 1,500 years to the early Church. In Acts 15, we find the Apostles calling together the first "church council meeting." The Gentiles were being added to the Church in noticeable numbers, which raised concerns regarding the Laws of Moses. The subject matter was whether or not the Gentiles had to obey Moses, which involves circumcision among other laws. Acts 15:1: *"And certain men which came down from Judea taught the brethren, and said, Except ye be circumcised after the manner of Moses, ye cannot be saved."*

I've been in church leadership for over 25 years and I can only imagine the dilemma which faced the Apostles. They had no New Testament! Jesus had promised them that the Comforter, which He would send to them, would lead them into all truth (John 14:26). Peter, Paul, Barnabas, and others had witnessed God working among the Gentiles, they being yet uncircumcised, which they rehearsed in the meeting. Please take the time to stop and read these passages for yourselves (Acts 15:7-12). This was a very interesting church council meeting.

Circumcision and Baptism

I don't know about you, but as a man, I can guarantee you that I would've been very interested in the outcome of that circumcision decision! Can you imagine what that would have done to the early Church, if circumcision would've been required to be saved? Circumcision started with Abraham and was carried into the Mosaic Covenant according to God's command. It was a "covenant mark" on the believer.

The Apostle Paul tells us in Romans 4:10-11, that Abraham was deemed righteous before he was circumcised, and that circumcision was *"a sign of the faith he had, yet being uncircumcised."* Paul goes on to show us the New Testament fulfillment of circumcision, in Colossians 2:11-12, where we find that we are *"circumcised with a circumcision made without hands,"* when we were buried with Him in our baptism! Water baptism is the New Testament fulfillment of Old Testament circumcision! I know, "water baptism is an outward show of an inward change," I hear that all the time, and it is true, but water baptism is so much more than that!

Water Baptism

Water baptism is not one of my topics for this book, but I will say this: in my baptism, the name of the Lord is invoked upon me, the temple of God, my heart is circumcised in a *"circumcision without hands."* My baptism places a "covenant mark on my life." I'm likened unto His death, burial, and resurrection, and the Holy Spirit coming upon me in power is directly tied to my water baptism, or at least it should be! I'm not "saved" by water baptism! Only the shed blood of Jesus has the power to save me and guarantee me eternal life. When I repent and receive the Lord as my Savior, the Holy Spirit regenerates me, saves me: Colossians 1:13, *"translates me out of the kingdom of darkness, into the kingdom of His dear Son."* That's what *must* happen to be saved. In my baptism, the same Holy Spirit comes upon the believer in power. That's the pattern in Scripture, e.g. the Holy Spirit came upon Jesus in His baptism! In Acts 19:1-7, we see Paul met some disciples (believers), and during their conversation, Paul asked them whether or not they had received the Holy Spirit since they believed. Upon finding out that they had not, Paul asked them what kind of baptism did they get? They responded that they had received John's baptism, and Paul tells them that they had to be baptized in the name of Jesus Christ.

Why did the Apostle immediately tie their water baptism with receiving the Holy Spirit? Verse 5-7 says, *"When they heard this, they were baptized in the Name of the Lord Jesus. And when Paul had laid his hands upon them, the Holy Ghost came on them; and they spake with tongues, and prophesied. And all the men were about 12."*

In the story of Peter and Cornelius, which we will cover later, I have to add this concerning water baptism: when Peter saw that God had given them the Holy Spirit, what is the first thing he does? He baptizes them! That's the only time in the New Testament that God gave the Holy Spirit to a believer apart from water baptism. Maybe it's because God knew Peter would not have baptized Cornelius apart from circumcising him first! However, even more importantly, Peter knew that water baptism and the coming of the Holy Spirit in power "agree." Therefore, when he saw that the uncircumcised Gentiles had received the same Holy Spirit as they did, he immediately takes them to water! Okay, off the rabbit trail — let's get back on course.

Peter and Cornelius

Now, let's look a bit more at the story of Peter and Cornelius, the Roman (Gentile) centurion (in charge of 100 men) in Acts 10. Verse 2 describes Cornelius as a *"devout man, and one that feared God with all his house, which gave much alms to the people and prayed to God always."* In verse 3-8, we see that Cornelius saw the *"angel of God"* in a vision and was told to *"send for one named Peter who was staying in Joppa at Simon the Tanners house."*

Peter's Trance

In the meantime, Peter goes up on the roof to pray in Joppa about the *"sixth hour,"* and in verse 10-16 we see that Peter was hungry and while they prepared food for him, Peter fell into a trance and saw Heaven opened and a sheet being let down. On the sheet were every sort of unclean beast, *"creeping things,"* for example, pork, octopus, shrimp, etc., which were considered unclean according to the Levitical Laws, which Peter was raised under (in the Bible, there are categories of various things, usually food, that God allows [clean] or denies [unclean] His people).

Then a voice from Heaven says, *"Rise Peter, kill and eat."*

To which Peter replied, *"Not so Lord, for I have never eaten anything that is common are unclean."* Then the voice spake again the second time, *"Call thou not common are unclean, what I have cleansed."* This was repeated three times!

Verse 17 says that while Peter was pondering what this meant, the three Gentile men sent from Cornelius were at the door seeking him. Verse 19-20 says, *"While Peter thought on the vision, the Spirit said unto him, behold, three men seek thee. Arise therefore, get thee down and go with them, doubting nothing: for I have sent them."*

Hmm, the sheet full of unclean things three times. Hmm, the voice saying *"call thou not common are unclean what I have cleansed"*! Hmm, three Gentile men at the door! Is God trying to get a message across to His Apostle? Do you think? So–o–o, Peter gets it! And he follows these three Gentiles to a Roman centurion's house. However, in his apparent reluctance Peter made sure he brought along a few of his friends (Jewish-Christian brothers) to witness this strange undertaking.

Peter's Arrival

Acts 10:24 says that when Peter arrived, Cornelius had gathered his household and was waiting on Peter to arrive. Cornelius falls down to worship Peter, then Peter quickly gets him up and tells him that he is also just a man! Peter also reminds Cornelius how it is unlawful (in Mosaic Law) for him, a Jew, to be in company with a Gentile, but God had shown him not to call common or unclean what He had cleansed. Cornelius then rehearses his story of how he was praying and an angel of God had appeared to him and told him to send for Peter, which he had done. Then Peter begins to preach the gospel to those gathered.

While he was yet speaking verse 44-48 says the Holy Ghost *"fell on all them which heard the word."* And the Jews which came with Peter were astonished, blown away, amazed, as they heard the Gentiles speak with tongues, and magnify God.

Peter then says, *"Who can forbid water that these be not baptized, which have received the Holy Ghost as well as we."* Peter takes an unprecedented step and baptizes these uncircumcised Gentiles for the first time! Wow, what a move. What a risk. As Peter said, *"How can we not"* baptize them, they received the Holy Ghost, the same as we did.

The Gentile Conflict

In other words, God knew that Peter's Jewish upbringing and understanding of the Law would not have allowed him to baptize an uncircumcised Gentile!! Thank God for visions! Thank God for the Holy Spirit given to lead them into truth! The New Testament was being written while there was much difficulty in the Church. If we read on in chapter 11:1-17, we find that when the other Apostles and brethren at Jerusalem heard that Peter had baptized the uncircumcised, they were not happy. Scripture says they *"contended"* with Peter and even *"separated themselves from him in a hostile way."* In the Amplified Bible in Acts 11:2, it says, *"So when Peter went up to Jerusalem, the circumcision party [Jewish Christians] found fault with him — separating themselves from him in a hostile spirit — opposing and disputing and contending with him."* Like I said, they were not "happy campers." Peter goes on to rehearse the whole experience with them and concludes his story with verse 17-18 when he basically says, "Who was I to resist God? He gave them the same Holy Spirit as He gave us when we believed, yet being uncircumcised." Then Peter's opponents *"held their peace"* but the fight wasn't over yet!

Truth Being Revealed

It is no wonder Peter wrote in 2 Peter 1:12 that he wanted the believers to be *"established in present truth."* Truth was being revealed, "is being revealed." I don't believe there is any "new truth," but I do believe that God is revealing and unfolding "the truth" which has been written! In other words, we can only "find" what has been there all along! Proverbs 25:2 says, *"It is the Glory of God to conceal a thing, but the honor of kings is to search out a matter."* He does not conceal a thing to keep us from finding it, but to cause us to put forth effort! To study! To read! To pray! He loves revealing His Word to His children. *"Seek and ye shall find. Knock and it shall be opened unto you."* I think it's important to say, "I believe the Bible to be the inspired Word of God, it was completed and closed prior to 70 AD, it contains absolute truth, and it is our final authority for what we believe!"

A few facts to consider: the Bible was written over a 1500 year period of time, by 40 different authors, on three continents, in three languages, yet it has a common theme (the creation, the fall, and the redemption of man) with no historical errors or contradictions! Tell me of another book that even comes close to those stats! Surely, everyone should read "that" best seller! By the way, regarding the "70 AD thing", I'll be all over that one in my topic concerning the dating of the writing of Revelation, so be patient, please ...

Amos's Prophecy Applied

Okay, so let's jump forward to Acts 15:7 and we see Peter gets up in the first church council and rehearses his whole experience regarding Cornelius. Then in verse 12, we see Paul and Barnabas get up and declare the signs, wonders, and miracles that God had worked through them among the Gentiles. Then James, the brother of Jesus, gets up in verses 13-18 and ties in the Old Testament prophecy of Amos 9-11, *"After this I will return and will build again the Tabernacle of David, which is fallen down; and I will build again the ruins thereof and I will set it up; That the residue of men might seek after the Lord, and all the Gentiles, upon whom my name is called, saith the Lord, who doeth all these things."* You see, James applies the rebuilding of the Tabernacle of David as beginning in his day! Obviously he was primarily referring to the coming in of the Gentiles, because David had Obed-Edom, a Gentile, as a doorkeeper. But if we look a bit closer at the Tabernacle of David, we see that David instituted music, singing, dancing, clapping, and every sort of instrument that was available to him. He even created musical instruments to be used. David used everything available to him, in his day, in worship of the Lord! There's no doubt, if David had had special-effects lighting, big full-color screens, computer-generated images, and smoke machines in his day, he would've used them as well to glorify God and create a worship atmosphere!

In David's order of worship, there were prophetic words spoken, clapping, dancing, and shouting. A lot of the psalms were written there as a result. In psalms 47:1 it says, *"O clap your hands all ye people, shout unto God with a voice of triumph."* A church worship service can be a noisy place at times and that's a good thing!

Being a Worshiper

While he kept the sheep as a young boy, David was a psalmist and a worshiper before the Lord in the field. He caught God's attention just being a faithful worshiper. Much later in history, Jesus was speaking to a Samaritan woman regarding worship, in John chapter 4, verse 23, *"But the hour cometh, and now is, when the true worshipers shall worship the Father in Spirit and in truth: for the Father seeketh such to worship Him.".* If you're a worshiper, God will seek *you* out! That's what He did with David, then He brought him out of the sheepfold and obscurity into greatness and kingship.

Later, David slew Goliath with God's help and, still later, King Saul would ask David to come and play his instrument of music when an evil spirit would vex Saul (see 1 Samuel 16:23). David would play and then the evil spirit would depart from Saul. David knew that the anointing could flow through music in a tangible way. Scripture never said that David sung a word. He played his instrument and deliverance came to the king. Music, in my short life has grown exponentially in its reach and quality. I remember about 25 years ago, my wife and I went to a live taping of the Army of God CD, which was being done by Integrity Music in Mobile, Alabama. Today, we are members of South Coast Church, which meets in that same building! The music, worship, and preaching at our church is cutting edge in Christendom and we fit right in.

Have you ever heard or partook in a worship song which was anointed? I do all the time! Whether in my truck with a good CD or at a church service. Music is a large part of what God has been doing in the rebuilding of David's order! I believe the time is coming and now is, when a worship team will no longer sing and play "about" healing, deliverance, and salvation; instead, they will sing and play, "healing, deliverance, and salvation"! The anointing on the team can flow into the atmosphere of the service in a tangible way and, as the congregation "gets on board," the anointing in the house is magnified, Christ is magnified, and where He is magnified, amazing and powerful things can and will happen.

Theological Flaws Regarding Music Today

Some churches today do not use musical instruments, that's not so bad, and such services *can* be anointed, but when they say you "should not" use musical instruments in church worship, that goes too far! As the Apostles were writing the New Testament, a lot of things changed from the Old Testament ways to the New Testament teachings and they let us know of the changes. For example, the priesthood changed (Hebrews 4:14-16), we are to pray in Jesus name (Colossians 3:17), we no longer offer animals blood for our sin (I Corinthians 5:7), baptism fulfills circumcision (Colossians 2:11-12), and so on. They *never* told us not to use musical instruments, plus, when you see James applying the reinstatement of the Tabernacle of David to the New Testament understanding, the evidence is clear, the theology of such critics is flawed. I didn't say they weren't saved! We *all* have flaws. Every church has flaws. I'm just applying good scriptural interpretation and seeking truth. May we be established in present truth!

A New Thing

I think it fair to say that "just because it's a new thing, does not guarantee it to be God." We should always put any "present truth" or "new thing" to the test. The scriptural test! The Apostles wrote the New Testament with the Old Testament, passing everything through the interpretive filter of the Cross, and witnessed by the Holy Spirit. You would be hard set to find one chapter in the New Testament which did not contain an Old Testament quote or reference! You see, the New Testament has been there all along, just veiled, until Christ came and the veil was removed (see 2 Corinthians 3:16).

Conclusion

We've heard a lot of theological ramblings about a rebuilt Mosaic Temple sometime in the future, however, nowhere in Scripture does it prophesy any rebuilding or reinstitution of the Mosaic sacrificial system. Note that the Lord Christ pronounced the destruction of the Temple worship system in Matthew 24! However, God, in Amos 9:11, prophesied the rebuilding of the Davidic order, not the Mosaic order! In Isaiah 16:5, we find another mention of the Tabernacle of David to consider. *"And in mercy shall the throne be established: and he shall sit upon it in truth in the Tabernacle of David, judging, and seeking judgment, and hasting righteousness."* Sounds like the Davidic Order is here for the long haul and you don't have to look far to see it.

David's Uniqueness

Of all the great people in the Old Testament, David stands out uniquely. About 14 chapters in the Bible speak of Abraham's life story, about 10 chapters regarding the life of Elijah, Joseph about 14 chapters, but David is written about in approximately 65 chapters of the Bible. There are about 1200 references to David's name in the Bible, 59 of these references are found in the New Testament!

If you think about a person of faith, Abraham comes to mind. If we think about a man of miracles, we think of Elijah; if we think about a dreamer, it's Joseph. But if we look for a man in the Old Testament known for praise and worship, it's David, hands down, no competition for that spot!

David operated as prophet, priest, and king, during his life. Now's that's also a big deal and it's not exactly in line with Old Testament protocol. If you were going to be a priest, you had to be of the tribe of Levi, if you were going to be a king, you had to be of the tribe of Judah! David ministered before the Lord in a priestly garment! He was king! And he wrote many prophetic scriptures throughout the Psalms. Again, we see David seeing where God was headed, 1500 years ahead of time! David was a picture of the Lord Christ's prophet, priest, and king ministry.

Okay, I think that will suffice regarding the Tabernacle of David. I'm sure the subject will surface again periodically as we continue down this road. In no way have I completely covered this topic and it's worth a study standing alone.

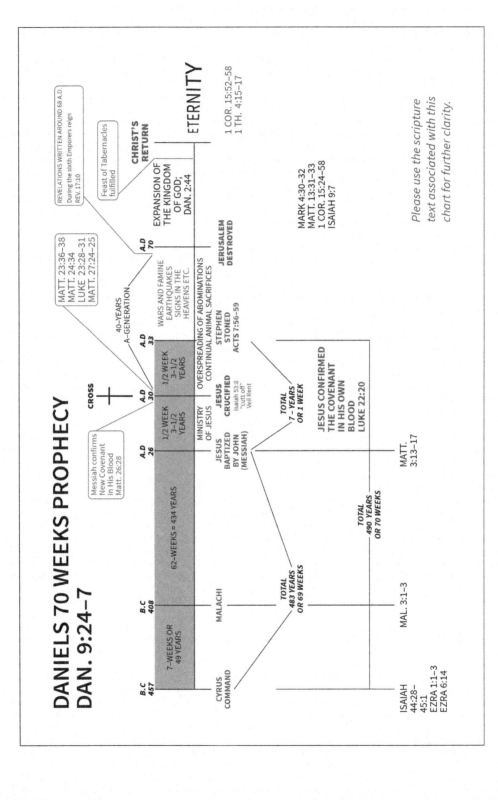

DANIELS 70 WEEKS PROPHECY
DAN. 9:24–7

CROSS

CHRIST'S RETURN

ETERNITY

Messiah confirms New Covenant In His Blood Matt. 26:28

MATT. 23:36–38
MATT. 24:34
LUKE 23:28–31
MATT. 27:24–25

REVELATIONS WRITTEN AROUND 68 A.D.
During the sixth Emporers reign
REV. 17:10

Feast of Tabernacles fulfilled

1 COR. 15:52–58
1 TH. 4:15–17

EXPANSION OF THE KINGDOM OF GOD;
DAN. 2:44

JERUSALEM DESTROYED

MARK 4:30–32
MATT. 13:31–33
1 COR. 15:24–58
ISAIAH 9:7

| B.C 457 | B.C 408 | A.D 26 | A.D 30 | A.D 33 | A.D 70 |

7–WEEKS OR 49 YEARS

62–WEEKS = 434 YEARS

1/2 WEEK 3–1/2 YEARS

1/2 WEEK 3–1/2 YEARS

40–YEARS A–GENERATION

WARS AND FAMINE EARTHQUAKES SIGNS IN THE HEAVENS ETC.

OVERSPREADING OF ABOMINATIONS CONTINUAL ANIMAL SACRIFICES

MINISTRY OF JESUS

JESUS CRUCIFIED
Isaiah 53:8
"cut off"
Veil Rent

STEPHEN STONED
ACTS 7:56–59

CYRUS COMMAND

MALACHI

JESUS BAPTIZED BY JOHN (MESSIAH)

TOTAL 483 YEARS OR 69 WEEKS

TOTAL 7 – YEARS OR 1 WEEK

TOTAL 490 YEARS OR 70 WEEKS

JESUS CONFIRMED THE COVENANT IN HIS OWN BLOOD
LUKE 22:20

ISAIAH 44:28–45:1
EZRA 1:1–3
EZRA 6:14

MAL. 3:1–3

MATT. 3:13–17

Please use the scripture text associated with this chart for further clarity.

Daniel's 70-Weeks Prophecy

Introduction

I know, I hear ya, "Daniel's 70-weeks prophecy again!" Calm down, it is fantastic! I guarantee that this topic will open your understanding. It is not that difficult to understand when it's taught properly and fits the whole of Scripture. And, it's historically accurate! I studied both the premillennial and post-millennial views of Daniel's 70 weeks and was amazed at what I saw. The premillennial view is what I was raised under, unknowingly, in my Southern Baptist upbringing. This is a good place for me to make this declaration: "I thank God for my Southern Baptist upbringing, I was taught the virgin birth, that the Bible is the inspired Word of God, that Jesus is my only hope of being saved, and many other great and important things. I met Jesus Christ there, was saved, and baptized." Okay, you get my point! I do not disdain my heritage. Just the opposite, I'm grateful for it! However, I have not "set up camp" there. Hebrews 11:10, *"For he looked for a city which hath foundations, whose builder and maker is God."*

Later in life, as I began to seek out the truth in God's Word on a much more intense level, I found myself driven to search, read, dig, pray, ask, etc. My theology has undergone some awesome changes and will continue to be adjusted as God continues to open my understanding. But, in this life, I will never have a complete handle on the truth! Romans 11:33, *"O the depth of the riches both of the wisdom and knowledge of God! How unsearchable are His judgments, and His ways past finding out."* Boy, what a ride!

Overview of Daniel

If you will read in the first part of Chapter 9 in Daniel, verse 2 says that Daniel understood that the 70 years of Babylonian captivity prophesied by Jeremiah in Jeremiah 25:11 was accomplished. You can then go on to read how Daniel prayed to the Lord and confessed his and his people's sin. Then in verse 21, the angel Gabriel appears to Daniel and gives him the "70-weeks prophecy." It's important to say that Gabriel is *always* connected with Messianic prophecies; he also appeared to Mary. So the first point I want to make is this is a Messianic prophecy! It's about the coming of Messiah. Also, for a bit of help as we start — a "week" here

17

in this scripture is speaking of 7 years. That is a well-known and agreed upon conclusion by all theological views, regarding Daniel's 70 weeks. Therefore, we know 70 weeks is 490 years of time being unfolded in response to Daniel's prayer. Also note, Gabriel gives us a "starting point" for this time frame to begin/

Here's the text, so let's read it through to start (Daniel 9:24-27):

Seventy weeks are determined upon thy people and upon the holy city, to finish the transgression, and to make an end to sins, and to bring in everlasting righteousness, and to seal up the vision and prophecy, and to anoint the most Holy. Know therefore and understand, that from the going forth of the commandment to restore and to build Jerusalem, unto the Messiah the Prince, shall be seven weeks, and three score and two weeks: the street shall be built again, and the wall, even in troublous times. And after three score and two weeks shall Messiah be cut off, but not for Himself: and the people of the prince that shall come shall destroy the city and the sanctuary; and the end thereof shall be with a flood, and unto the end of the war desolations are determined. And he shall confirm the covenant with many for one week: and in the midst of the week he shall cause the sacrifice and oblation to cease, and for the overspreading of abominations he shall make it desolate, even until the consummation, and that determined shall be poured upon the desolate.

I know, that was a mouthful! I'm telling you again, this is an awesome prophecy! Before I begin to break it down for you, I want to refer you to a chart that I've prepared, to help you understand the prophetic time frame given. I usually make fun of charts, as my past experience has seen charts that proved to be wrong. Most of them were all about predicting the return of Christ, which Christ Himself clearly said, "No man shall know the time," but in opposition to my own past dislike of charts, I took the time to produce this chart in an effort to help my readers understand the 70-weeks prophecy. This chart in no way predicts the return of our Lord, although it clearly predicts the first advent of our Lord. The prophecy of Daniel has been so messed up by some teachers that we all could use some help, so give the chart a shot, it is not difficult to understand.

Things To Be Accomplished in That 490 Years

Note that at the very outset of the prophecy, Gabriel gives a list of things to be accomplished within this 490 years or 70 weeks. The list is *"to finish the transgression, and to make an end to sins, and to bring in everlasting righteousness, and to seal up the vision and prophecy, and to anoint the most Holy."* It's immediately evident, especially considering that we're looking back at history, that Christ alone accomplished this list! Just before He "gave up the ghost," He said, *"It is finished."* Then after He rose, He ascended to His Father and is now seated at the right hand of God and has anointed the *"most holy"* in heaven!

Cyrus

Take a look over the chart for a moment as I explain a few things. We know that we are dealing with a total of 70 weeks or 490 years of time. The starting point is the *"issuing"* of the command to restore and build Jerusalem, which King Cyrus did around 457 BC. On that note, I have to show you Isaiah 44:28 and 45:1, *"That saith of Cyrus, <u>He is my shepherd</u>, and shall perform all my pleasure: even saying to Jerusalem, Thou shalt be built; and to the temple, Thy foundation shall be laid. Thus saith the Lord to <u>His anointed,</u> to Cyrus, whose right hand I have held, to subdue nations before him; and I will loose the loins of kings, to open before him the two leaved gates; and the gates shall not be shut;* Isaiah prophesied this almost 200 years *before* King Cyrus was born! That's clearly a God thing!

Josephus

I found in Josephus an interesting read concerning Cyrus. Josephus was a Jewish historian hired by the Romans to write an historical account of the wars, prior to 70 AD's destruction of Jerusalem. In addition to writing what all he witnessed around 70 AD, he also did an overview of Jewish history dating all the way back to the creation.

Concerning Cyrus, he writes in Book XI, chapter I, "In the first year of the reign of Cyrus, which was the seventieth from the day that our people were removed from their own land into Babylon, ... God stirred up the mind of Cyrus, and made him write this throughout all Asia: Thus saith Cyrus the King, since God Almighty hath appointed me to be King of the habitable earth, I believe He is that God whom the nation of the Israelite s worship; for indeed He foretold my name by the prophets, and that I should build Him a house at Jerusalem, in the country of Judea. This was known to Cyrus by his reading the book which Isaiah left behind him of his prophecies ... Accordingly, when Cyrus read this, and admired the divine power, an earnest desire and ambition seized upon him to fulfill what was so written." Now that's cool! Someone in authority brought King Cyrus the book of Isaiah where God calls Cyrus, who was a heathen king, *His Shepherd, His anointed!!* and calls him by name some 200 years before! Good stuff! The king is so taken back by it that he makes the declaration we just read and begins the process of releasing the Jews to go back and rebuild the city and the sanctuary.

I find in Ezra chapter 1, verse 1-2, a similar reference to Cyrus: *"Now in the first year of Cyrus king of Persia, that the word of the Lord by the mouth of Jeremiah might be fulfilled, the Lord stirred up the spirit of Cyrus king of Persia, that he made a proclamation throughout all his kingdom, and put it also in writing, saying, Thus saith Cyrus king of Persia, The Lord God of heaven hath given me all the kingdoms of the earth; and he hath charged me to build him a house at Jerusalem, which is in Judah."* Okay, so the time has started with King Cyrus issuing the decree around 457 BC, and that begins the 70 weeks or 490 years.

The Temple Rebuilt

Another Scripture reference pertaining to the rebuilding of Jerusalem is found in Nehemiah 4:16-17, which shows that they built the walls in *"troublous times."* The Scripture literally says they worked with one hand while the other hand held a sword.

69 Weeks unto Messiah

I noticed that Gabriel breaks down the first 69 weeks into *"seven weeks and threescore and two weeks."* The first seven weeks or 49 years brings us to the writing of Malachi, the last book of the Old Testament. Then there was over 400 years of "silence" from God until a wild haired, locust eating prophet named John busted onto the scene six months ahead of Messiah, to prepare the way of the Lord.

By the way, a "score" is twenty, so, three score and two weeks is 62 weeks, which added to the first 7 weeks equals 69 weeks *"until the Messiah"* or 483 years, which brings us to the time of Jesus being baptized by John in the Jordan River and the Holy Spirit descending upon Him ! Boom! He became the Messiah, the anointed, the Christ, in His baptism, and began His three and one half years of miracle-working ministry. (For clarity regarding Jesus "becoming the Messiah" in His baptism, the literal interpretation of the word "Messiah" is "Anointed one." The Holy Spirit descended upon Jesus immediately following His baptism and abode upon Him. In addition, He did no recorded miracles in the Bible until after His baptism. In a way, He was the Messiah from birth, but His Messianic ministry with signs and wonders following did not begin at His birth.) Near the end of that time, Jesus confirms the New Covenant "in His own blood." Jesus said in John 26:28, *"For this is my blood of the new testament [covenant], which is shed for you."* He is the one who confirmed the covenant! The prophecy is about Him!!

Midst of the 70ᵗʰ Week

That brings us to the midst of the 70th week, when Christ is crucified, *"cut off."* In Isaiah 53, we find very familiar Scripture passage concerning the Messiah, in verse 8, *"He was taken from prison and from judgment: and who shall declare His generation? For he was <u>cut off</u> out of the land of the living: for the transgression of my people was he stricken."* I love it when the Bible gives me the clarity I'm needing when interpreting it. I'm not talking about pulling Scripture "out of context" to support a flawed belief system! Isaiah 53 is a Messianic prophesy; it contains information regarding Christ's ministry, rejection, and crucifixion. It is "in context"!

Jesus was crucified at Passover, by the way (no coincidence!), and God rent the veil of the Temple. Mark 15:37-38, *"And Jesus cried with a loud voice, and gave up the ghost. And the veil of the Temple was rent [torn open] from top to bottom,"* which He did to signify the *"cessation of animal sacrifices."* Christ is the "He" who confirmed the covenant! Christ is the "He" that *"caused the sacrifice and oblation to cease"!* This prophecy is *not* about the antichrist! It's about Jesus Christ! The end of the 70th week is the stoning of Stephen, which happened 3.5 years after Christ was crucified. Stephen was the first Christian martyr, and his death began the "persecution of the Church," which became so bad that within a generation, Nero, the Roman emperor, *ordered* the persecution of Christians, and cooperated with the Jews in doing so. This persecution continued until Rome then turned on the Jews and *"burned her with fire"* (Revelation 17:16). Uh oh, I just opened another can of worms. I'll leave that one alone for now, got to continue with Daniel.

Overspreading of Abominations

In the middle of verse 27, it says *"and for the overspreading of abominations he shall make it desolate."* This refers to the destruction of Jerusalem and the Temple sacrificial system, which destruction came in 70 AD — within that very generation! Most scholars agree that the Roman armies' encircling Jerusalem in the 70 AD siege is the best interpretation of this verse. I agree with that interpretation.

Jesus specifically warns His disciples regarding this in Matthew 24:15-21, *"When ye therefore shall see the abomination of desolation, spoken of by Daniel the prophet, stand in the holy place, (whoso readeth, let him understand:) Then let them which be in Judea flee into the mountains: Let him which is on the housetop not come down to take any thing out of his house: Neither let him which is on the field return back to take his clothes. And woe unto them that are with child, and to them that give suck in those days! For then shall be great tribulation, such as was not since the beginning of the world to this time, no, nor ever shall be."* Also, note the Lord's words in Luke 21:20-22, *"And when ye shall see Jerusalem compassed with armies, then know that the desolation thereof is nigh. Then let them which are in Judea flee to the mountains; and let them which are in the midst of it depart out; and let not them that are in the countries enter there into. For these be the days of vengeance, that all things which are written may be fulfilled."* The Lord is clearly speaking of something sudden, which can easily be seen as the Roman armies coming upon and surrounding Jerusalem.

However, I can't help but notice the words *"overspreading of abominations"* in the text, which gives a sense of ongoing or continuing abominations, in

22

the plural. On that note, Isaiah 66 comes to mind, which helps us see what the Lord defines as an "abomination" in His sight. The whole chapter is a must-read, but I want to home in on verse 3, *"He that killeth an ox is as if he slew a man; he that sacrifices a lamb, as if he cut off a dog's neck; he that offereth an oblation, as if he offered swine's blood; he that burneth incense, as if he blessed an idol. Yea, they have chosen their own ways, and their soul delighteth in their abominations."*

These various offerings were all ordained by God in the Mosaic Covenant and were a crucial part of worship. How is it that God, in this prophetic text, considers such offerings to be an abomination? It's quite simple — after the Lord Jesus shed His blood for the sin of the world, it would be an abomination in the sight of God for anyone to offer the blood of an animal for their sin. After God rent the veil in the Temple from *"top to bottom"* as His Son died on the Cross, the Jewish leadership eventually "put it back together" and continued with animal sacrifices until the 70 AD destruction. I imagine, for one thing, their job security was at stake! A 40-year "overspreading" or continuing of abominable animal sacrifices, until the Roman armies besieged the city for four months, which was the culmination of abominations, and then destruction came! The coming of the Roman armies obviously was the sudden event the Lord warned His disciples of, but many of Christ's followers, no doubt, viewed animal sacrifices (along with other tenets of Judaism) as an abomination and an enemy of Christ.

A Commonly Taught Error

In premillennial theology, they teach that the 70th week of Daniel is "removed" from the consecutive prophecy and placed somewhere in the future! Do what? They have *no* authority from Scripture to do such a thing! Daniel's prophecy was given as a consecutive prophecy! Gabriel gave no reason to break the last seven years off and throw it somewhere ambiguously in the future! Then to top that off, premillennial theology sometimes injects "antichrist" as the *"he"* who *"confirms the covenant,"* and also the *"he"* that causes the *"sacrifices and oblation to cease"*! That's why they must teach a rebuilt Mosaic Temple, complete with animal sacrifices in the future, in order for the 70th week to "be" fulfilled. Oh, and they say the

70th week of Daniel coincides with the seven-year tribulation. Wow, what a mess, I hope the "lights" just came on for you!

That's right! Nowhere in Scripture does it prophesy any rebuilt Mosaic Temple and animal sacrifices. I think it would be a blasphemy to shed animals' blood as a cover for our sin, when the *"Lamb of God"* has shed His blood for our sin! Christ Himself pronounced the total destruction of the Old Testament Temple sacrificial system! So, if they find the "ashes of the red heifer," make movies about the Ark, and even if books are written about premillennialism by Christians who buy into these things, I've decided to stay with clear Scripture, which does *not* support such a belief!

Conclusion

The 70-weeks prophecy of Daniel was a consecutive prophecy, the subject was the coming Messiah, confirming the New Covenant in "His own blood," being "cut off," and causing the sacrifice and oblation to cease. The prophecy also ends with language regarding the destruction of the Temple sacrificial system and Jerusalem, which happened within that generation, as the Lord Christ said it would, in Matthew 24:34, *"Verily I say unto you, This generation shall not pass, till all these things be fulfilled."*

I think the 70-weeks topic has been touched upon enough for now. I'm sure this topic will also pop up here and there as we continue with this book. It's interesting that Daniel's primary focus of his prayer was for his people to return to Jerusalem and their way of life, as prophesied by Jeremiah. But the answer he got went far beyond his request, all the way to the coming of the Messiah and the end of animal sacrifices, along with the destruction of the Temple and Jerusalem. By the way, the three wise men who came seeking Him who was born to be the King of the Jews, were from Mesopotamia and no doubt had Daniel's 70-week prophecy available to them, which they used to help them when they saw the "star" that they followed. Remember, Daniel was a captive and wrote his prophecies in Mesopotamia.

The Feast of
Tabernacles

The Feast of Tabernacles

This is probably my favorite topic on the list for this book. I began looking at the feasts of Israel about 25 years ago. What I have found is highly treasured in my heart, as it has shown me a bit clearer image of the beautiful picture God has painted and is continuing to reveal to us.

The first scripture I want to bring to your attention is Psalm 89:15. I've read it from several translations and found the Amplified Bible to open my understanding best, so here it is: *"Blessed, happy, fortunate (to be envied) are the people who know the joyful sound (who understand and appreciate the spiritual blessings symbolized by the feast): They walk, O Lord, in the light and favor of your countenance!"*

Now concerning whether or not we should study the feasts of Israel, I rest my case! Who wouldn't want to *"walk in the light and favor of the Lord's countenance"*? This will be fun.

Old Study Notes

I found some of my old study notes and Scripture references on the feasts of Israel, from a quarter century ago. The computer paper still has the perforated edges running down each side and the several pages are still one long piece of paper, about six feet long. Guess I never took the time to separate all the old, perforated pages. Oh well, I'll leave it as is now, it's cool, my progeny will really think it's cool one day, if it's still around. I still have several handwritten study notes of my grandfather's (Clarence Sprinkle), along with his concordance and pastor's manual. Priceless stuff. Maybe my family will treasure the old printouts about Israel's feasts.

Let's start with the Lord's Word concerning celebrating the feasts in the Old Covenant (Deuteronomy 16:16): *"Three times a year shall all thy males appear before the Lord Thy God in the places which He shall choose: in the Feast of unleavened bread (Passover), and in the feast of weeks (Pentecost), and in the feast of tabernacles: and they shall not appear before the Lord empty."* Jerusalem became the place of the Lord's choosing and all Israel would gather at Jerusalem to celebrate the feasts throughout their history.

I think it's important to say that, as Christians, we no longer are expected to celebrate the "literal" feasts of Israel. I do know of many Christians who observe the Jewish feasts in our day, some are Messianic congregations (Jews who have received Christ as Messiah), and I have no issue with the continued celebration of the feasts of Israel, other than animal sacrifices, however, I believe the spiritual symbolism is where the meat is! Also, as I will show with Scripture and history, the Feast of Passover and the Feast of Pentecost have been fulfilled. Only the Feast of Tabernacles remains unfulfilled in our day — it's the greatest of all the feasts and comes at the end of the harvest season!

The Feast of Passover

Historically we find that the first Passover (also known as the Feast of Unleavened Bread) took place in Egypt. Exodus chapter 12 gives us the story. God told Israel to take an unblemished lamb and *"strike"* its blood on the doorposts of their houses, cook and eat the lamb with unleavened bread, so that the Lord's death angel would *"pass over"* their houses and not slay their firstborn. Exodus 12:13 says, *"And the blood shall be for you a token upon the houses where ye are: and when I see the blood, I will <u>pass over</u> you, and the plague shall not be upon you to destroy you, when I smite the land of Egypt."*

This feast was celebrated for some 1,500 years, as the fulfillment was waiting on Christ's crucifixion (Christ was crucified during the Feast of Passover (see I Corinthians 5:7, where Scripture says, *"For even Christ our passover is sacrificed for us"*). The Feast of Passover was clearly fulfilled at the crucifixion of our Lord. Christ became our Passover Lamb, His blood on us causes God's judgment against sin to "pass over" us because He sees the blood. Only the blood of Jesus redeems us, saves us, and guarantees us eternity in heaven! Not water baptism nor baptism in the Holy Spirit nor the gifts of the Spirit. Water baptism along with spirit baptism prepare us to live "this life" to its full possibilities, it equips us for "this life." The blood prepares us for the next life! The thief on the cross did not need water nor spirit baptism, as he was about to die! He only needed the blood applied, which Christ did.

Feast of Pentecost

In history, the first Pentecost was at Mt. Sinai when Moses got the Ten Commandments and the Mosaic Covenant (the Covenant of Law) was established. It is also called the Feast of Weeks because it was 7 weeks and 1 day or 50 days after Passover, Pentecost meaning "fifty." You can read the whole story regarding the first Pentecost in Exodus, chapters 19-32. God not only gave Moses the Ten Commandments, but also gave him instructions for building the Tabernacle of Moses, the duties of the priesthood, and various other laws. When Moses came down the mountain, he found the people worshiping an idol; Moses called for those who were on the *"Lord's side"* to gather to him. Then in Exodus 32:28, *"And the children of Levi did according to the word of Moses: and there fell of the people that day about three thousand men."*

So, we see, at the first Pentecost, three thousand died, at the giving of the Law. Now let's move forward about 1,500 years and we come to Acts 2:1, *"And when the day of <u>Pentecost</u> was fully come."* The early church was all gathered and had been praying and waiting on the promise of the Father that Jesus said would come. Luke 24:49, *"And, behold, I send the promise of my Father upon you: but tarry ye in the city of Jerusalem, until ye be endued with power from on high."* Jesus told them this after He had resurrected from the dead and after He had said, in John 20:22, *"He breathed on them, and saith unto them, receive ye the Holy Ghost."* On that note, I must remind us that the Apostles had received the Holy Ghost (indwelling, rebirth) prior to being told to tarry for the *"promise of my father."* Therefore, the promise of His Father was a baptism of the Holy Ghost and power, which came 50 days after He was crucified. God intentionally waited until the Feast of Pentecost to "fulfill" it by the promise of Holy Ghost "power" coming upon the believers. In our day, there's no need to *"tarry"* for the Holy Ghost. If so, then you must stay "true" to the entire text and *"tarry at Jerusalem"*!

A new convert should be saved, baptized, and filled with the Holy Ghost and Power as soon as possible — there's no reason to wait! Peter didn't wait! Paul didn't wait! I'm not saying that you "will not" necessarily tarry, pray, and wait for the Holy-Spirit-power baptism. That's up to the Lord on each individual basis, but if we stay true to the patterns in Scripture on this subject, there's no requirement to wait in our day!

How Many Were Saved that Day?

When the Holy Ghost came upon believers, Scripture says there was *"a sound of a rushing mighty wind, and it filled all the house where they were sitting . . . and Cloven tongues of fire sat on each of them, and they all spake with tongues as the Spirit gave them utterance"* (Acts 2:2-4). Very similar sights and sounds were at the first Pentecost at Mount Sinai. Scripture goes on to say that men from every nation were gathered at Jerusalem for the feast and when they all heard the commotion, they gathered around the early church and claimed that these men were drunk.

Then Peter gets up and basically says, "It's only 9:00 in the morning. These people are not drunk as you suppose" and he preaches his first sermon of the New Testament upon which Acts 2:41 says "about 3,000 souls" were added unto the church! At the first Pentecost 3,000 died and at the fulfillment of Pentecost 3,000 were saved —that's no coincidence! The giving of the Law brought death and the giving of the Holy Spirit brought life! Again, we see that God knew exactly what He was doing all along. Has it ever occurred to you, that nothing has ever occurred to God?

Rain

In Old Testament Israel, God would send an actual "early rain" upon the barley crops of Israel and they would bring in an "early harvest," and as part of the feast celebration they would wave the barley loaves (Leviticus 23:20). Remember, the feasts of Israel were very much to do with agricultural harvest. The Feast of Pentecost was an early barley harvest.

The symbolism represented in the first two feasts is easy to see, primarily because we are able to "look back" at their fulfillment in

Christ's crucifixion and the coming of the Holy Spirit in power, 50 days later. Okay, we'll leave Pentecost alone for now — I think enough has been said for where I'm taking us.

Yet To Be Fulfilled

There is still one feast yet to be fulfilled, the Feast of Tabernacles. It was the greatest feast of all and it came in the seventh month, at the end of the harvest season. God would send an "early and later rain" upon the crops of Israel, and they would bring in the corn, wine, and oil. It was a time of in-gatherings. Hosea 6:3 says, *"Then shall we know, if we follow on to know the Lord: His going forth is prepared as the morning, and He shall come unto us as the rain, as the latter and former rain unto the earth."* We also notice in the New Testament book of James, chapter 5, verse 7, *"Be patient therefore, brethren, unto the coming of the Lord. Behold, the husbandman* [the farmer] *waiteth for the precious fruit of the earth, and hath long patience for it, until he receives the early and later rain."* James is using his understanding of the agricultural feasts of Israel to support his statement. We also note: at the time of James writing, he was still looking for a much greater "rain" to come and the sure harvest that would follow, as he uses references akin to the Feast of Tabernacles, regarding the rain which God would surely yet send! Jesus said in the parable of the tares and wheat that *"Harvest was the end of the world"* (Matthew 13:39).

I've heard some folks say that because Christ was probably born somewhere near the Feast of Tabernacles, that He fulfilled it at His birth. That just doesn't work! Why would God reverse the order that He established and fulfill Tabernacles first? In addition, I see no historically fulfilled symbolisms in that opinion that fits Scripture nor history. And why would the Apostle James reference the early and later rains as "yet to come" in the New Testament. Enough said! The Feast of Tabernacles is yet to be fulfilled in the future!

Conclusion

The early rain of the Spirit at Pentecost in Acts 2 has brought about the spread of the Kingdom of God to where it is today. The revivals, signs, and wonders over the past 2,000 plus years, along with the exponential growth of Christianity are the results and these things are ongoing in our day! What Jesus started 2,000 years ago, with 12 disciples by His side, has grown to the point of dominating the planet. Christianity has the most believers of all religions on planet Earth today and it's still growing!

It's exciting to imagine the results of a "flood of rain," "former and later rain," together coming upon the end-time Church. There will no doubt be revivals, miracles, signs, and wonders like never before and a great "God" harvest will be the results. Therefore, we can stand firm and say again, "The greatest days are ahead."

All right, we'll leave the Feast of Tabernacles for now as we move on to the next topic.

Dating the Writing
of Revelation

Dating the Writing of Revelation

I hear you, "What's important regarding when Revelation was written?" Glad you asked, and the answer to that question is forthcoming.

Being raised under premillennial theology, I was taught that Revelation was written some time around 90 AD under Domitian's reign. The reason for that date is that it fits well with premillennialism's teaching that all the apocalyptic language in Revelation is yet to be fulfilled *in the future*. However, if Revelation was written prior to the 70 AD destruction of Jerusalem, premillennialism's teachings regarding futuristic fulfillment appear to be bankrupt! The date of the writing of Revelation is very important, as we will see.

The Bible Is the Best Interpreter of the Bible

Remember, one of the main interpretive methods we should use is the Scripture itself, where possible. Let's look at Revelation 17:9-10, *"And here is the mind which hath wisdom, The seven heads are seven mountains on which the woman sitteth. And there are seven Kings: five are fallen, and one is, and the other is not yet come; and when he cometh, he must continue a short space."* John is writing this during the sixth emperor's reign. I don't need a Ph.D. to see that, when John says *"five are fallen, and one is,"* it's obvious that John is writing this during the sixth king or emperor's reign. Nero was the sixth, does the number six mean anything in Revelation? Duh! Nero was a beast of a man, he murdered his own mother, he would dress up as a beast and sexually molest young men, he was the first emperor to order the persecution of Christians, and he ultimately ordered the destruction of Jerusalem, but he did not live to see it happen because he committed suicide in late 68 AD. Therefore *according to Scripture*, Revelation was written prior to the destruction of Jerusalem. And Nero was no doubt the personification of 666, the beast, the man of sin! Nero's name in the Hebrew language is numerically represented by 666. That changes everything theologically regarding our future view!

The Caesars

Regarding the Revelation 17:9-10 scriptures, the line of Caesars/emperors/kings is as follows: Julius, Augustus, Tiberius, Caligula, Claudius, Nero, and Galba. Galba only ruled about six months, which again fits the

Scripture, a *"short space."* On the same note, 69 AD was known as the "year of four emperors." After Nero committed suicide in late 68 AD, they had Galba, Otho, Vitellius, and Vespasian in power as Caesars or Emperors during 69AD. There was total upheaval in the known world. *"There shall be wars and rumors of wars,"* Jesus said in the Matthew 24. Trouble was building up throughout the years which lead up to the 70 AD destruction.

Context

The book of Revelation was written to the seven churches of Asia Minor, which are each named at the start of the book. Revelation was to be read in the churches, and it was! If I was a member of one of those early churches around 68-69 AD, and they read the book of Revelation in our church service, which named our church as one to whom it was written, I would have had a clear reason to believe that I would experience everything written. That's "context." Revelation was written to them, in that day and therefore it pertained to them! If I may ask, "Why would God have a book like Revelation written to the seven churches of Asia Minor, if it primarily pertained to some generation thousands of years in the future?" I don't think so!

For a complete exposition of Revelation, I would highly recommend a great book *Days of Vengeance*, by David Chilton. Chilton does an awesome exposition on Revelation, which I will not spend much time on for the purpose of this book. My main purpose for looking at the date of the writing of Revelation has been accomplished. It was written prior to the destruction of Jerusalem in 70AD!

Conclusion

Revelation was written prior to 70 AD, during Nero's reign, which lasted from 54-68 AD. Revelation was written to the seven churches of Asia Minor, warning them of events which would *"shortly"* and *"quickly"* take place! The events of Revelation regarding beast, tribulation, and destruction were historically fulfilled in the first century! That takes the "air" out of premillennialism's futuristic fulfillment teachings. Maybe, the church would stop looking like a constant negative prognosticator, who is continually proven wrong, if we see these things as historically fulfilled! If we're looking for the futuristic fulfillment of all these terrible events, it's easy to see why everything from the birthmark "on Gorbachev's head to a possible computer glitch (Y2K) can be seen as possible signs of the end times." Wrong viewpoint!

The Olivet
Discourse

This sermon of Jesus is generally referred to as the Olivet Discourse, due to the fact that Jesus sat down on the Mount of Olives and gave this discourse to His followers. This is a great topic with varied theological opinions regarding the words of our Lord as He is nearing His crucifixion. He speaks His final words of judgment to the religious leaders, the Temple and Jerusalem, followed by words which depicted a terrible time ahead for that generation to go through.

Interpretive Principle

A great interpretive principle to use is to move from the clear Scripture to the obscure during your interpretation efforts. I've studied theological opinions which bypass clear Scripture and build their belief system around obscure Scripture — that's backward methodology. We must also consider "context" (who was the book written for, who was Jesus speaking to), and always remember, the Bible is the best interpretive tool we can use. The Lord periodically gives us keys within Scripture to open and understand His words.

As always, I highly recommend that you stop here, and read the Olivet Discourse in Matthew 23-24, Mark13, and Luke21. Go read it ...

Context

Let's start our analysis with context. The Lord had just gone through an exchange which ended with "woes" to the religious leaders and Jerusalem.

Matthew 23: 33-38 says, *"Ye serpents, Ye generation of vipers, how can ye escape the damnation of hell? Wherefore, behold, I send unto you prophets, and wise men, and scribes: and some of them ye shall kill and crucify; and some of them shall ye scourge in your synagogues, and persecute them from city to city: That upon you may come all the righteous blood shed upon the earth, from the blood of righteous Able unto the blood of Zacharias son of Barachias, whom ye slew between the temple and the altar. Verily I say unto you, <u>All</u> these things shall come upon <u>this generation</u>. O Jerusalem, Jerusalem, thou that killest the prophets, and stonest them which are sent unto thee, how often would I have gathered thy children together, even as a hen gathereth her chickens under her wings, and ye would not! <u>Behold your house is left unto you desolate.</u>"*

Cleansing the Temple

In Malachi 3:1, it says, *"And the Lord, whom ye seek, shall suddenly come to His Temple."* We know from Scripture that Christ cleansed the Temple in the beginning of His ministry in John 2:16, when He referred to it as *"my Father's house,"* and He did so again near the end of His ministry, as recorded in Matthew 21:13, where He refers to the Temple as *"my house."* Then, after His final "war of words" with the religious leaders, He referred to the Temple as *"your house"*!

The Beauty of the Temple

As we continue into chapter 24 of Matthew, we see that Jesus "departs" the Temple and His disciples came to Him to show Him the beauty of the Temple building. I imagine they were trying to "talk Him down," so to speak. Then Jesus replies, in verse 2, with His prophecy concerning the Temple's utter destruction: *"And Jesus said unto them, See ye not all these things? Verily I say unto you, There shall not be left here one stone upon another, that shall not be thrown down"*. We see here, that Christ Himself pronounced the destruction upon the Temple and Jerusalem.

The Discourse

Then Jesus went and sat down on the Mount of Olives and His disciples came to Him and asked Him privately in verse 3, *"Tell us, when shall these things be? And what shall be the sign of thy coming, and of the end of the world (age)?"* You can go check for yourselves, the proper translation is "age" not "world." It was the Old Testament "age" which was ending, not the "world." Most other translations use the English word "age," which better fits the original text.

From there, the Lord begins telling them of wars and rumors of wars, false prophets, famines and earthquakes. He also said in verse 21, *"For then shall be great tribulation, such as was not since the beginning of the world to this time, <u>no, nor ever shall be.</u>"* He continues with other signs they were to expect, then in verse 34 He gives them a clear key of interpretation regarding who would experience all these things: *"Verily I say unto you, <u>This generation shall not pass, till all these things be fulfilled.</u>"*. There's a key! He was speaking to them in that day!

And He told them that "their" generation would not pass until all these things would be fulfilled! Now that I've been given a clear key, I must view the passage as being fulfilled in that generation! In Luke 23, verses 27-31, as Jesus was carrying His Cross to be crucified, it says, *"And there followed Him a great number of people, and of women, which also bewailed and lamented Him. But Jesus turning unto them said, Daughters of Jerusalem, weep not for me, but weep for <u>yourselves and your children</u>. For, behold, the days are coming, in the which they shall say, Blessed are the barren, and the wombs that never bare, and the paps which never gave suck. Then shall they begin to say to the mountains, Fall on us; and to the hills, Cover us. For if they do these things in a green tree, what shall be done in the dry?"* Again, we see Jesus warning "that generation" of the terrible times they would face.

Other Arguments

I know, I've heard the arguments that Jesus was speaking of the Jewish race when He referred to the generation which would not pass away until these things be fulfilled. Not so!! Go look it up for yourselves. Here' are references in the New Testament where the same Greek word *genea* is also used: Matthew 1:17; 11:16; 12:39, 41, 42, 45; 16:4; 17:17; 23:36; 24:34; Mark 8:12, 38; 9:19; 13:30; Luke 1:48, 50; 7:31; 9:41, 11:29, 30, 31, 32, 50, 51; 18:8, 17:25, 21:32. Not *one* time is it speaking of the Jewish race! It always refers to "the sum total of those living at one time" and it's always "contemporary." I guarantee you, the disciples and women who heard Him say what He said, believed "they" would live to see all those things! And history proves they did! Josephus records a story in book VI, chapter IV, paragraph 4, of women within the walls of Jerusalem, during the siege, who cooked and ate the own children, due to starvation.

Difficult Text

A lot of what Jesus said is rather difficult for us to accept as historical because we weren't there as witnesses, and due to our limited understanding of Old Testament prophetic language concerning judgments from God. We do know from history that the Roman Empire, which ruled the habitable known world around AD 70 had fallen into upheaval and chaos; Nero committed suicide in late 68 AD, then the next Caesar/king was Galba, who only ruled about six months and was murdered by a Roman guard. Then in 69 AD, Rome had three more Caesars/kings, Otho, Vitellius, and Vespasian. There was total "upheaval" in the world power center, Rome, leading up to 70 AD!

Eyewitness Account

This is a good place for me to quote some of Josephus's writings, as he was there, and made an historical record of the events. Josephus, book VI, chapter V, paragraph 3 (speaking about false prophets that had risen up) says, "Thus were the miserable people persuaded by these deceivers, and such as belied God himself; while they did not attend, nor give credit, to the signs that were so evident, and so plainly foretold their future *desolation*; but, like men infatuated, without either eyes to see nor minds to consider, did not regard the denunciations that God made to them. Thus there was a *star resembling a sword, which stood over the city, and a comet, that continued a whole year*."

Famine

Josephus was there! Jesus said there would be "signs in the heavens." Josephus records earthquakes in Judea which killed over 10,000 men! Again, a key given to us is that all these things He spoke of would come upon that generation of the first century. If we look in Acts 11:28, *"And there stood up one of them named Agabus, and signified by the Spirit that there should be a great dearth (famine) throughout all the world: which came to pass in the days of Claudius Caesar."* Claudius Caesar ruled just before Nero. All the terrible things Jesus had warned them about were happening and intensifying, as they lead up to the 70 AD destruction, which came on that generation! A generation is commonly considered to represent about 40 years. Jesus gave the Olivet Discourse around 33 AD and in 70 AD, almost 40 years later, the destruction came. Over 1,100,000 people died within Jerusalem's walls, in four months! And over 96,000 were taken captive. That's not to mention the tens of thousands killed all over Israel, the Sea of Galilee, and so forth in various battles. The walled city of Jerusalem would not normally contain over 1,200,000 people but when the people saw the Roman armies coming, they all ran into the supposed safety of the walled city. Big mistake. That's why the Lord had warned His followers to "get out" of the city!

Difficult Text to Consider as Historically Fulfilled

If you read the whole of the Olivet Discourse, you should have noticed some difficult scripture to consider in an historical context regarding its fulfillment, I know I did! As we consider the difficult text, I remind us of two things:

1. Always move from the clear to the obscure or unclear.
2. Stay true to the scriptural keys that are clear.

Remember the key that Christ gave us in verse 34 of Matthew 24: *"This generation shall not pass till all these things be fulfilled"*?

One of the difficult texts is found in Matthew 24:29-31 which reads, *"Immediately after the tribulation of those days shall the sun be darkened, and the moon shall not give her light, and the stars shall fall from the heaven, and the powers of the heavens shall be shaken: And then shall appear the sign of the Son of man in heaven: and then shall all the tribes of the earth mourn, and they shall see the Son of man coming in the clouds of heaven with power and great glory. And he shall send his angels with the great sound of a trumpet, and they shall gather together his elect from the four winds, from one end of heaven to the other"* (KJV).

Staying true to Scripture, we must deal with the first word, which says "Immediately" after the tribulation of those days! So Jesus is telling them they would see these things take place immediately following the tribulation! Can't get away from "Immediately"!

Prophetic Vocabulary

In our day, we would think Jesus is saying that He would be returning immediately following the tribulation, but we know from history that Christ has not yet returned, therefore we look closer. The language Jesus is using to describe the destruction of Jerusalem, the Temple, and the Old Covenant ending in the establishment of His Kingdom is "prophetic vocabulary." He continues using the same prophetic vocabulary to describe the "light of Israel" being extinguished as a covenant nation.

The world as they knew it would end! The Old Covenant would be abolished. Let's look at a few Old Testament scriptures which use the same prophetic language as we also stay with the "rule of first mention" in our methodology. The rule of first mention is an interpretive method which traces a particular subject or phrase through Scripture, beginning at its first use, in our effort to understand it.

The Lights Are Going Out

When Isaiah was prophesying the destruction of Babylon by the Medes, he said in Isaiah 13:9-10, *"Behold the day of the Lord is coming, Cruel, with fury and burning anger, to make the land a desolation; And He will exterminate its sinners from it. For the stars of heaven and their constellations will not flash forth with their light: The sun will be dark when it rises, and the moon will not shed its light."*

When Ezekiel predicted the destruction of Egypt he writes in Ezekiel 32:7-8, *"And when I extinguish you, I will cover the heavens, and darken their stars; I will cover the sun with a cloud, And the moon shall not give its light. All the shinning lights in the heavens I will darken over you and will set darkness on your land."*

We know that none of these events literally took place. God never intended us to view His remarks as literal in these passages! But these things all did happen, as the lights went out on these wicked nations! The prophetic language brings a bit of understanding to the Lord's words; He was saying that Israel as a covenant nation would cease to exist, the "lights" were going out! In John 1:11, concerning our Lord, it says, *"He came to His own, and His own received Him not."* Instead they crucified the Lord of Glory.

The Sign of the Son of Man

Now for the next difficult part of the text, I will quote David Chilton's book, *Paradise Restored*, as I believe he did an excellent job.

Regarding Matthew 24:30, a word-for-word rendering from the Greek actually reads "And then will appear the sign of the Son of Man in heaven."

As you can see, two important differences come to light in the correct translation: first, the location spoken of is heaven, not just the sky; second, it is not the sign which is in heaven, but the Son of Man who is in heaven. The point is simply that this great judgment upon Israel, the destruction of Jerusalem and the Temple, will be the sign that Jesus Christ is enthroned in heaven at the father's right hand, ruling over the nations and bringing vengeance upon His enemies. The divinely ordained cataclysm of AD 70 revealed that Christ had taken the Kingdom from Israel and given it to the Church; the desolation of the old Temple was the final sign that God had deserted it and was now dwelling in a new Temple, the Church.

I note that Chilton did no harm to Scripture and actually used what is written to bring understanding. He also stayed true to the key the Lord gave us!

Old Testament Reference to "Coming in the Clouds"

Another difficult text addresses the Son of Man coming in the clouds. Let's also look at what has been written using the same descriptive language.

In Daniel 7:13-14, we find an Old Testament reference regarding the Son of Man coming in the clouds: *"I saw in the night vision, and, behold, one like the Son of man came with the clouds of heaven, and came to the Ancient of days, and they brought him near before him. And there was given Him dominion, and glory, and a kingdom, that all people, nations, and languages, should serve him: his dominion is an <u>everlasting</u> dominion, which shall <u>not pass away</u>, and his kingdom that which shall <u>not be destroyed</u>."*

Two New Testament scriptures also fit in well:
Acts 1:9, *"And when He had spoken these things, while they beheld, He was taken up; and a cloud received Him out of their sight."*
Mark 16:19, *"So then after the Lord had spoken unto them, he was received up into heaven, and sat on the right hand of God."*

The above Scripture references help me to see that Matthew 24:30 was not speaking of Christ's second coming to the Earth, but His ascension to the right hand of His Father. He will remain there until His enemies have been made His footstool. The most-quoted Old Testament scripture in the New Testament is Psalm 110:1, *"The Lord said unto my lord, Sit thou at my right hand, __until__ I make thine enemies thy footstool."*

The Gathering of His Elect

Another difficult text which had to be looked at carefully is Matthew 24:31: *"And He shall send His angels with a great sound of a trumpet, and they shall gather together His elect from the four winds, from one end of heaven to the other."*

When I first read this verse, years ago, during my premillennial upbringing, this event was the "rapture." However, we know that the "rapture," in fact, did not take place in "that generation"! Remember, the "key"! Jesus said, *"This generation shall not pass till all these things be fulfilled."*

If we look closer, we find the word "angels" is commonly used for messengers or preachers of the Gospel. Referring to John the Baptist, in Matthew 11:10 (*"For this is he, of whom it is written, Behold, I send my __messenger__ before thy face, which shall prepare thy way before thee"*), the Greek word translated as "messenger" is often translated as "angel"! There are many other references regarding the same word being interpreted as a messenger. Let's look at one more in Luke, where the Lord sent messengers ahead of Himself to make ready the people to receive Him in a Samaritan village. Luke 9:52, *"And [He] sent __messengers__ before his face: and they went, and entered into a village of the Samaritans, to make ready for him."*

Gather

The word translated as *"gather"* is commonly interpreted as "synagogue." Many of the early Christian congregations called themselves "synagogues." Jesus even uses the same word in Matthew 23:37-39, when He is lamenting over Jerusalem, their rejection of Him, and the resulting destruction He knew would shortly come. Then in verses 37-39, He says, *"O Jerusalem, Jerusalem, thou that killest the prophets, and stonest them which are sent unto thee, how often would I have __gathered__ (synagogue) thy children together, even as a hen __gathereth__ (synagogues) her chickens s under her wings, and ye would not! Behold, your house is left unto you desolate."*

Conclusion

If we stay true to Scripture, history, good interpretive methodology, and if we stay with the scriptural interpretive keys which are given, we can see our understanding opened. Jesus was saying that *"immediately following the tribulation of those days,"* which climaxed at the total destruction of the Old Covenant Temple, the lights were going out on Israel as the covenant nation of God. Jesus would rule from heaven, at the Father's right hand, and His messengers would go out and "synagogue" His elect together. The total destruction of the Temple, "blew the trumpet" for the Church (synagogue) of Jesus Christ, and heralded the Church as the new Temple, indwelt by the Holy Ghost. This process has been ongoing, and will continue until it fills the earth. Scripture says in Isaiah 58:1, *"Cry aloud, spare not, lift up thy <u>voice</u> like that of a <u>trumpet</u>."* The early Church Apostles and leaders were accused of having *"turned the world upside down"* in Acts 17:6, with their doctrine concerning one Jesus, whom they reported to be King.

Again, I have not by any means covered every detail of the Olivet Discourse, but I've found enough understanding to help me see it as an historical event, fulfilled in the first-century generation, as the Lord said it would be.

The Rock

The Rock

In Daniel 2, we find the story of Nebuchadnezzar, the Babylonian king, who had a dream which Daniel interprets. You should stop and read chapter 2 in Daniel first — it's an interesting read to say the least. There has been a lot of wrong interpretations regarding this dream, because some commentators do not see it as historical in its complete fulfillment. Somehow, they have taken a dream consisting of four kingdoms and stretched it into our day. Let's take a look together.

In the first several verses, we see that Nebuchadnezzar had a dream and the king was greatly troubled by his dream and wanted his wise men in Babylon to not only give him an interpretation of the dream but also to tell him the dream itself, without first hearing it from the king ... smart king!

Obviously, the wise men could not do what the king asked, so Nebuchadnezzar ordered all the wise men of Babylon to be killed. Daniel, being one of them, sought the Lord and got the answer! In verse 29 on down, Daniel tells the king what he dreamed and what it meant.

The king had seen a great image, which consisted of a *"head of gold"* that Daniel said was king Nebuchadnezzar himself. Then he saw the *"breast and arms of silver,"* which we know from history was the Medo-Persian Empire, which defeated the Babylonians. Then the *"belly and thighs were of brass,"* which history also tells us was the Greek Empire, which defeated the Persians. Then finally, the king saw *"legs of iron, his feet part of iron and part of clay."* Again, we know from history, that the legs could represent the Roman Empire which defeated the Greek Empire.

Notice, Daniel only mentions four kingdoms! Now we're getting to the good part, in verse 34-35 Daniel says the king saw a *"stone was cut out without hands, which smote the image upon his feet"* and the image was destroyed and blown away *"like the chaff ... and the stone which smote the image became a great mountain, and filled the whole earth."* That was the dream, then Daniel gives the king the interpretation, beginning in verse 37-45.

The Interpretation

After Daniel tells the king exactly what the king had seen in the dream, Daniel begins the interpretation by telling him, in verse 38, *"Thou art this head of gold."* Therefore, we know that king Nebuchadnezzar was the beginning of this image. Then Daniel goes on to tell the king that an *"inferior"* kingdom would come after him, which we know to be the Medo-Persian Empire which defeated Babylon. He then goes on to tell the king about the third and fourth kingdoms which would also come. History again tells us that represented the Greek and Roman kingdoms. The Roman Empire was known to be divided into ten provincial kingdoms, which the ten toes represented.

Again, it is important to realize that there were "only" four kingdoms total. How some teach that this prophesy regarding the iron and clay legs and feet stretches to our day in its fulfillment is beyond my understanding. The only part of this prophecy which is continuing in our day is the "rock," which is continuing to fill the whole earth!

We know that Christ, "the Rock," came on the scene during the Roman Empire and that Christianity eventually saw the conversion of Emperor Constantine to Christianity (he ruled the Roman Empire from 306 to 337 AD). Theodosius I who ruled from 379-395 outlawed paganism and made Christianity the state religion. Not long afterward the, Roman Empire fell, never to rise again! Now for verse 44-45, *"and in the days of these kings shall the God of heaven set up a kingdom, which shall never be destroyed: and the kingdom shall not be left to other people, but it shall break in pieces and consume all these kingdoms, and it shall <u>stand forever.</u> Forasmuch as thou sawest that the stone was cut out of the mountain without hands, and that it brake in pieces the iron, the brass, the clay, the silver, and the gold; the great God hath made known to the king what shall come to pass hereafter: and the dream is certain, and the interpretation thereof sure."*

No man shall ever again rule the habitable earth, except for Christ Jesus. And His kingdom will *"fill the whole earth."* Hitler tried it, Muhammad tried it, along with a few others, to no avail. All the misguided teaching about some "antichrist" becoming a world leader, along with a "one-world government", is rubbish! There will never be any man who will rule the habitable Earth, except the man Christ Jesus!

The Foundation Is Built

All right, now that we've laid a solid foundation, which follows Scripture and is historically correct as well, I have several things to say with biblical confidence. So, hold on, because you will be challenged to view the future of our world in a much greater way than before. I feel no need to store up food, money, or ammunition. I'm not moving to a remote location to survive the "terrible things" that are coming. Jesus specifically prayed in John 17:15, *"I pray not that thou shouldest take them out of the world, but that thou shouldest keep them from the evil"* ... sorry, my greatest hope is not escape!

My Upbringing

I was raised under and met the Lord in a premillennial Baptist church. Not to mention, dispensational teachings were "ramped up." Dispensational teachings, which firmly got a grip on conservative Baptist, Methodist, and even Pentecostal churches in my day, is about 170 or so year's old. Dispensationalism started with a woman named Margaret MacDonald, in Glasgow, England, around 1830. She was 15 when she reportedly had a vision of the saints of God being raptured before the tribulation. Then John Nelson Darby picked up Margaret's vision and ran with it. It wasn't long before C.I. Scofield got a hold of Darby's teachings and charts, and the Scofield Reference Bible was published. It was filled with footnotes, opinions of the author, and out-of-context quotes, which supported a flawed belief system. I would call that a "new teaching"! But it does not pass muster with Scripture, nor with history!

I remember all their charts, showing the different dispensations, and by the year 2,000, the chart ran out! It was going to be all over with! Oh well, I imagine they have made new charts since I was a kid. The Scofield Bible sold over ten million copies and is still in print today! By the way, if you look up the meaning of the word "dispensation" in the Greek language, it has nothing to do with a time frame or period of time. It has to do with "stewardship." For example, we know that Paul was given the dispensation of grace to the Gentiles, which means that the stewardship of the Gospel of grace to the Gentiles was given to Paul. The very word "dispensation" has been wrongly used to represent various time frames of God's plan throughout history. God has never dealt with man on the basis of dispensation. He has always dealt with man on the basis of covenant!

A Bankrupt Theology

Dispensational theology is bankrupt, in my opinion, and I have watched it dying a slow death during my lifetime — it's "on the ventilator" but still around. I remember several dispensational books being written and I'll mention two: *88 Reasons Why Christ Will Return in 1988*, by Edgar C. Whisenant, and *The Late Great Planet Earth* by Hal Lindsay has sold over 15 million copies. Lindsay believed that because Israel became a "nation" again in 1948, the generation living, would see the return of Christ, which had to happen, no later than 1988 (a generation, 40 years). I read those books and they were wrong! They were based on a wrong view of Scripture! They failed to apply it in an historical context! I might add, to my knowledge, none of them have apologized, nor offered a refund! Believe it or not, I'm trying hard to be "nice" about this. The intention of my book is not to attack dispensationalism nor the carious authors of books on that subject, but I had to "drop a bomb" where needed!

Terminal Generation

Why is it that a lot, if not all, of the various generations have a tendency to see themselves as the "terminal generation"? I myself can deal with the likelihood that I will be dead, buried, and well on my way back to dust before the Lord returns. But He will surely return and raise my dead body back to life. On that note, I must say, I am a three-part person, body, soul, and spirit. Most of my life, I've heard it taught that "you are a spirit, who lives in a body, and has a soul." Sorry, I have to disagree with that quote. I am body, soul, and spirit, and God will raise me body, soul, and spirit! Christ is my only example of the "resurrected man" and He was raised body, soul, and spirit! We were made in the image of God, and He is three persons, yet one. God the Father, God the Son, and God the Holy Spirit. Three yet one!

A Few Crazies

As of today, I firmly believe the greatest days are ahead, for the Kingdom of God, the Church, humanity, and the whole of creation! We have had, and will continue to have, a few crazies raise their heads up, only to see them lopped off by the "sword of the Lord." The Lord Christ alone "is" and "will" rule all things, not to mention planet Earth!

Terrorists

As I write this, Islamic terrorists have killed 14 people and injured many others, in San Bernardino, California, during a Christmas Party. And terrorists have also killed over 130 people in Paris, France, about two weeks earlier. Radical Islam's goal is the "take over" of planet Earth, through the spread of Islam and enforcement of its tenets. People who believe otherwise will be killed. This takeover attempt is not new in my day. Study the 7th-century wars of Muhammed, their "prophet." Such events may continue a few hundred more years, for all I know, but one thing is sure: the Kingdom of Christ alone will stand forever. Islam, along with every other religion which does not accept the teachings of Jesus, that He was "God in the flesh," Emanuel, will come to naught!

The Islamic state cannot fight with developed nations on a "toe-to-toe" basis. Thus, we have terrorism, the only weapon they can use in their efforts to further their cause. I found an interesting statistic in *Mega Shift* (by James Rutz): "More Muslims have converted to the Christian faith over the past ten years than have over the past one thousand years." Hmmm, that's interesting! Winston Churchill did not hold anything back, when he said "Islam is as dangerous in a man as rabies in a dog." Don't sound like Winston was a politically correct politician, which is a big problem in our day! Okay, my book is not written to attack Islam, nor any other religion, only to proclaim the Gospel of Jesus Christ. It just happens to be "current events" in my world today!

Historical Context

All the terrible events in Revelation, along with the Olivet Discourse, were historically fulfilled! I'm looking for the Kingdom of our Lord, to continue filling all things. The "leaven is working in the flour, but has not yet leavened the whole barrel" (Luke 13:21), the "mustard seed has been planted in the Garden, but has not yet filled the garden" (Luke 13:19), Christ's enemies are "dropping like flies," but they have not all yet become His footstool (Psalm 110:1)! There will be "tares" in the wheat field of the Earth, until Christ returns, but remember, the world is a wheat field, not a tares field! The Lord Christ was the "seed" planted in the Earth, and it has and will "bring forth much fruit" (Matthew 24:13-30)!

I live with great hope and expectation for the future! I encourage my family and friends with my outlook! I have "good news" to preach, and I do! By the way, a footnote: if you read the parable of the tares and wheat in Matthew 13:24-30, you can't get away from the fact that the tares were gathered up and burned *first*, before the wheat was gathered into the barn. Uh oh, did that hit a nerve? Good. Dispensational premillennialism tells us to expect to be "raptured" off this Earth prior to the Lord's return. This teaching came into play during the onset of dispensational teachings, however, Scripture does not support any "rapture" of the saints prior to the Lord's return. In Matthew 13:41, Jesus said *"The son of man shall send forth His angels, and they shall gather out of His kingdom all things that offend, and them which do iniquity."* Also, in Proverbs 2:22, it says *"But the wicked shall be cut off from the earth, and the transgressors shall be rooted out of it."* And in Matthew 5:5, Jesus said *"Blessed are the meek: for they shall inherit the earth."* Now the Matthew 13: 24-30 parable mentioned above makes sense, when it says that the tares will be gathered *first* and burned!

I'm reminded of a quote by a dear friend of mine, Andrew Shearman, who said, "He is the Word, I am the voice, I have something to say, and I'm going to say it." I would say, my "driving force" to write this book fits Andrew's quote well. Recently, Andrew has come up with another good quote: "Don't come and go and nobody know." By the grace of God, that will not be the summation of my life! I'll be gone soon enough, but I'm not gone yet! So, I'll continue to say what I feel I have to say and pray that many will know I was here!

Technology

Technology is moving at such a fast pace in my life and I think technology can be used for the glory of God. Today we have hot and cold running water, air conditioning, cruise control, cell phones, computers, and the internet. Medical technology is also moving at an exciting pace, which brings hope for healthier and longer lives. We burn fuels much cleaner, we recycle our waste more and more, all of which reinforces my theology! Military technology is amazing; we are now flying war planes without pilots, using robotic devices to keep humans out of harm's way, satellite photos, and high-tech listening equipment. If I live a while, I may see a man walk on Mars! The fast-paced movement of technology also augments the theology I'm presenting.

The Ark of the Lord

I was excited to find out that the Ark of the Lord was moved into Solomon's Temple during the celebration of the Feast of Tabernacles in I Kings, chapter 6 and 8. That gives me another glimpse of what to expect during the fulfillment of the Feast of Tabernacles. The first Feast of Tabernacles to be celebrated was after Joshua led the children of Israel into the Promised Land! Again, a bit of insight! Today, we know from the New Testament that Christ is the "ark" of God and that He synagogues with His people all over the world, as they continue to spread the Gospel.

The day is coming when His presence and glory will fill the Church (the Temple) in such a way as not seen before — the Feast of Tabernacles! There will be unprecedented miracles, signs, and wonders in the future, the greatest revivals and the greatest harvest of souls. Jesus said in John 14:12, *"Verily, verily, I say unto you, He that believeth on me, the works that I do, shall he do also; and greater works than these shall he do; because I go unto my Father."* Sounds like the Feast of Tabernacles, sounds like early and later rain of the Spirit. Sounds like God knows exactly what He is doing. Looking at the Old Testament shadows gives us awesome insight to where we are headed. Again, we see that the greatest days are ahead!

Last Days' Prophecies

I do believe there are unfulfilled prophecies in our day which coincide with the Feast of Tabernacles, so I've decided to list a few here and comment on them. It's important when reading Old Testament prophecies, which have a future fulfillment, to understand a few very important interpretive tools, especially concerning Jerusalem, Zion, and the Temple. The New Testament gives us this interpretive tool in many ways, throughout the Scriptures. Paul sums it up in Hebrews 12:22-23: *"But you are come unto mount <u>Zion</u>, and unto the <u>city of the living God</u>, the <u>heavenly Jerusalem</u>, and to an <u>innumerable company of angels</u>, To the <u>general assembly and church of the first born, which are written in heaven</u>."* That's all in one breath! One sentence!

With that in mind, lets read Isaiah's prophecy, Isaiah 2:2-4: *"And it shall come to pass <u>in the last days</u>, that the mountain of the Lord's house shall be established in the top of the mountains, and shall be exalted above the hills; <u>and all nations shall flow unto it</u>. And many people shall go and say, Come ye, and let us go up to the mountain of the Lord, to the house of the God of Jacob; and he will teach us of his ways, and we will walk in his paths: for out of Zion shall go forth the law, and the word of the Lord from Jerusalem. And he shall judge among the nations, and shall rebuke many people: and they shall <u>beat their swords into plowshares, and their spears into pruning hooks: nation shall not lift up sword against nation, neither shall they learn war any more</u>."*

Sounds like the greatest days are ahead! Now for another prophecy written by Micah, which is almost word for word what Isaiah said, in Micah 4:1-3: *"<u>But in the last days</u> it shall come to pass, that the mountain of the house of the Lord shall be established in the top of the mountains, and it shall be exalted above the hills; and <u>people shall flow unto it</u>. And many nations shall come, and say, Come, and lets us go up to the mountain of the Lord, and to the house of the God of Jacob; and he will teach us of his ways, and we will walk in his paths: for the law shall go forth of Zion, and the word of the Lord from Jerusalem. And he shall judge among many people, and rebuke strong nations* *afar off; and they shall beat their swords into plowshares, and their spears into pruning hooks: nation shall not lift up a sword against nation, neither shall they learn war anymore."*

Do you think those two scriptures are filled with hope for the best days to come?

Life Expectancy

In my life, I've watched our life expectancy consistently rise. The average American is expected to live to 80 years old now! When I was born in 1956, the average life expectancy for men was 66.7 years. In 1900, the average was 46.3 years for men. Recent history clearly shows we are living longer and longer. If you read Isaiah 65:17-25, you can see the day coming when we will be living well over 100 years old! It says in verse 20 (Amplified Bible): *"There shall no more be in it an infant that lives but a few days, or an old man who dies prematurely, for the child shall die an hundred years old, and the sinner who dies when only a hundred years old shall be [thought only a child, cut off because he is accursed]."* The scripture is speaking of events which will come to pass prior to the Lord's return, as people are still dying in this text! When Christ returns, *"There will be no more death"*! This time of long life is yet ahead, and the passage goes on to say in verse 25, *"The wolf and the lamb shall fed together, and the lion shall eat straw like the ox; and dust shall be the serpent's food. They shall not hurt or destroy in all My holy Mount [Zion], says the Lord."* Hmmm, again, sounds like the greatest days are ahead! What else could we expect as the Gospel of our Lord continues to spread and change lives?

The "leaven" of the Gospel has and will permeate the whole of humanity. That permeation has and will effect governments, education, health, families, and will continue to bring about good stewardship of this Earth that we've been ordered to tend.

When I was young, the news often talked about "smog" and they would show pictures of the haze covering most big cities. I haven't heard anything regarding "smog" in decades now, other than China, due to all the manufacturing, along with vehicles and equipment which are not yet up to par. We have cleaned up our exhaust emissions and we continue to push forward with cleaner and cleaner ways to use our energy. As boat builders today, we are now required to use tier 3 certified engines in the tugs and fishing boats we are building. It started with tier 1, then tier 2, tier 3, and today the larger horsepower engines must be tier 4. These tier levels are EPA certifications regarding exhaust emissions. Today, we have ten times the vehicles burning fuel on our roads, rivers, and waterways as we did when I was young and no smog talk any longer. Again, technology proclaims the Glory of God! I know we still have air pollution issues to be dealt with, but I believe technology is helping us — and will continue to help us — in our stewardship of this planet.

How to Pray

The Lord's disciples had watched Him do miraculous things while they spent three and one half years with Him. They no doubt heard Him pray, and were so impressed with the power in His prayer, that one day, they asked him *"Lord, teach us to pray."* To which the Lord replies in Luke 11:2-4, *"When ye pray, say, Our Father which art in heaven, Hallowed be thy name. <u>Thy kingdom come. Thy will be done, as in heaven, so in earth</u>. Give us day by day our daily bread. And forgive us our sins; for we also forgive every one that is indebted to us. And lead us not into temptation; but deliver us from evil."* Although we commonly refer to this as "the Lord's prayer," it was actually the manner in which the disciples were taught to pray. Therefore, a better name would be "the disciple's prayer." As disciples, we are not told to necessarily repeat word for word what the Lord said, but to pray "in this manner." It's fine if we simply pray word for word what He said, but the point I'm making is this: He taught us the "manner" or "pattern" we are to employ while praying.

The first thing we learn is to approach our Father in a reverential manner. He is an awesome creator Father, who loves us more than we can fathom. Then we are to pray with two fundamental goals in mind: *"Thy kingdom come. Thy will be done, as in heaven, so in earth."* I can only hope you just caught that. No matter what we find ourselves praying about, we must establish our hopes on those two goals! Did the Lord actually expect His Kingdom to come and His will to be done? Apparently so. He wasn't a "negative prognosticator" regarding the future! And He wants us to have the same dream. I cannot believe for one minute that the Lord gave us a vain prayer. His Kingdom will fill the Earth and it will stand forever.

If Christ Reigns Now

I here ya, "If Christ reigns now, why aren't all nations converted and why is there so much evil remaining in the world?" First off, there's no question that Christ is seated at the right hand of the Father, ruling over all things. Christ's victory over Satan occurred in His death and resurrection and it has moved progressively throughout history as nation after nation is influenced by His finished work. Christ came to *"destroy the works of the devil."* That's what He did when He walked on this dirt for three and a half years of miracle ministry, and that's what He has continued to do through His Church ever since! Ultimately, His Kingdom will fill the Earth and God will have a great harvest! Heaven will have much more than hell. The Earth is God's wheat field! Christ is the seed and He is the Lord of the Harvest!

Closing Remarks

It seems like I could go on and on. The Scripture is filled with hope for the greatest days ahead for humanity, the Earth, and all of creation as the Gospel of Christ continues to spread and permeate every part of human existence. My greatest hope is not to escape, but to influence my world. One day, I will surely stand before my Lord and I take that thought very seriously! The only things I can lay before Him are the things I've done to bring glory to His great name! I tremble at the thought of my lack.

I've heard Christian folks talk about the crowns we will one day get. I, for one, could never wear a crown of any sort in His presence. Any crown that His grace may cause me to get, will be thrown down before His feet!

We have "good news" to share with our world. May I shout it from the rooftops. "Christ reigns," "His Kingdom is filling and will fill the Earth," "He paid a price no one else could have paid," we've been redeemed, set free, empowered, and employed for life in His service. Father, help me to become a better example of "God with skin on," filled with Your Spirit, attentive to Your voice, and empowered to do Your will. I love what my pastor, John Breland, says: "The way is narrow (which is Christ), but the life we are called to live is broad, abundant, and overflowing!" May we live a life that is attractive, which draws people to us, as they were drawn to Him. Sinners flocked to Him and were comfortable in His presence. May we be a "life source," in some way, to everyone we touch in this life. We have nothing to fear and everything to celebrate! May my worship of Him be Davidic in its "style" (singing, dancing, leaping, shouting, clapping, lifting my hands, self-abasing) and glorifying of His great name! How can we express our love and gratefulness for all He has done, and *not* make somewhat of a fool of ourselves for Christ's sake! Pride and fear of embarrassment be damned. I bow before His awesome majesty and welcome Him to examine my life daily. His response to me is always filled with forgiveness, love, and hope!

Now, let's get with the program. We have good news to share with a world in need. Notice, I did not say "a dying world" or "the devil's world." Psalm 24 says *"The earth is the Lord's, and the fullness thereof; the world, and they that dwell therein."* The devil owns nothing, he is a liar, a murderer, and a defeated foe. Our world is not dying! It's being renewed day by day and the "water of life" is flowing from the altar of God's Temple (the Church), bringing life to every dead thing! Isaiah 9:7 says, *"Of the increase of His government and peace there shall be no end."* Romans 1:17 declares, *"From faith to faith."* 2 Corinthians 3:18 says, *"From glory to glory,"* and Psalm 84:7 proclaims *"They go from strength to strength."* We have a front-row seat in this "feature presentation" of God's show. May we remove our "fogged goggles" and begin to see clearly, without fear, and filled with hope, for the greatest days are ahead!

CPSIA information can be obtained
at www.ICGtesting.com
Printed in the USA
LVOW13s2324190117

521600LV00008B/523/P